T0198797

ROMP IN ROOM

Debra Franceschini

iUniverse, Inc.
New York   Bloomington

Romp In Room

iUniverse books may be ordered through booksellers or by contacting:

iUniverse
1663 Liberty Drive
Bloomington, IN 47403
www.iuniverse.com
1-800-Authors (1-800-288-4677)

Because of the dynamic nature of the Internet, any Web addresses or links contained in this book may have changed since publication and may no longer be valid. The views expressed in this work are solely those of the author and do not necessarily reflect the views of the publisher, and the publisher hereby disclaims any responsibility for them.

ISBN: 978-1-4401-1283-6 (pbk)
ISBN: 978-1-4401-1284-3 (ebk)

Printed in the United States of America

iUniverse rev. date: 1/21/09

ROMP IN ROOM
SECTION I

SECTION I CONTENTS

BLUEBIRD PICTURE ACTIVITY

Curriculum Area: Language Arts

Objectives: This activity promotes socialization, helps with recognition of birds and builds an awareness of bird life. The activity invites children to respond to music and use of the large muscles in gross motor activity.

Materials:

- Large area for movement
- Pictures of a bluebird adhered to a bristle board for sturdiness

Procedure:

- Introduce the picture of a bluebird to the children
- Using any melody of a nursery rhyme, sing the lyrics to the song with the children to help them become familiar with the tune

> "Bluebird, Bluebird
> Out my window
> Bluebird, Bluebird
> Out my window
> Won't you come and play"

- Have the children listen to the song a few times before they start the action activity
- Hand clapping is an excellent way to learn music appreciation
- Pass the picture to each child so that they may have a close-up look
- From a circle with the children holding hands, have the children lift their hand over their heads to form a bridge
- One child is selected to be the bluebird
- Sing the words to the verse as the children begin the game
- The child that is selected will weave his or her way through the children's arms (under and over action)
- When the selected child has done all the actions around the circle, he or she will choose another child to take their place around the circle

Evaluation: When this activity is done the children should have a better concept of what a bluebird looks like. Children will display turn taking and socialization skills.

COMPARISON ACTIVITY
BIRD FEATHERS

Curriculum Area: Sensory

Objectives: This activity promotes the use of sense of touch and the child's awareness of
                texture. The children learn to classify different materials according to texture.

Materials:

- Small table and chairs
- Large group area
- Household materials such as cotton balls, silk, duster and fur pieces etc.
- Bird Feathers

Procedure:

- Have children gather around the table in groups of three or four
- Place the bird feather on the table
- Place several of the household materials on the table, discuss the comparisons
  of some of these soft items to the texture of the feather
- Pass the items around the table so that each child can feel them and compare
  the texture to the bird feather
- Ask the children questions (ie) does the cotton feel as soft as the feather
- Continue until all materials have been compared to the feather

Evaluation: Children will acquire an awareness of texture. They can discuss the difference
                between the feel of a feather to other animal coats or common materials. They
                will enjoy this activity as a hands-on experience.

BUSY BEE RHYME

Curriculum Area: Language Arts

Objectives: This activity introduces children to insects in a friendly way. They explore bees as living creatures and learn about their behaviors and habits. They will learn how bees walk and fly by observing a safe demonstration using a puppet.

Materials:

- You will need to prepare for this activity by making a simple "Busy Bee" puppet from a yellow balloon, some scraps of black felt and a little glue
- Yellow balloon
- Black felt (eyes, nose, stripes) make your bee using these materials before the lesson
- Large group area

Procedure:

- Have the children sit in a circle in the reading area
- Introduce your "Busy Bee" puppet
- Talk about the colours of the bee
- Have Busy Bee say hello to all the children
- Recite the Busy Bee rhyme to the children demonstrating the actions as you recite ----- Busy Bee, Busy Bee, always buzzing around me, Your work is so neat, your honey is a treat, so fly to your hive, and let your wings beat, until next we meet
- Have the children try to repeat the actions using hand gestures
- Repeat the rhyme several times until all the children are familiar with the actions

Evaluation: This activity will encourage the children to develop knowledge of bees and familiarize them with the insect species. It will facilitate new vocabulary by repeating the names of the insects, as well as words for their surroundings.

BUILDING A BEEHIVE

Curriculum Area: Science / Math

Objectives: A bee is one of the first insects a child discovers. The children will learn about the discovery of the insect and its habitat. The activity is a hands-on experience, encouraging children to explore.

Materials:

- Large area for block activity
- Assorted blocks in different colours
- Picture of a beehive

Procedure:

- Have children sit on the floor in the block area
- Allow them to choose different coloured blocks
- Encourage the children to build a beehive together, using the picture as an example for the shape, assist the children with the activity
- Have them leave a large open space in the middle of the beehive for the Busy Bee to fly in and out of
- When the children are done building the beehive let each one hold the Busy Bee balloon and pretend they are flying Busy Bee in and out of the beehive, be sure to make "buzzing sounds" with them

Evaluation: The activity combines math, gross motor skills and cognitive learning skills. The children will stack the blocks and you will find that some of the older children will attempt to put the blocks together. Since this activity uses an advanced concept (building) the teacher will have to assist the younger children.

EXPLORING THE OUTDOORS

Curriculum Area: Science / Social Studies

Objectives: This activity will encourage the children to have respect for all living things. The children will hopefully have the opportunity to see a live bee, which will help their awareness of insect life. They will use eye to hand coordination when using the magnifying glass. One of the more amusing areas covered will be the use of expressive language when and if they spot a bee.

Materials:

- Outdoors (the best area would be a garden)
- Magnifying glass

Procedure:

- Take the children outside to a garden area
- Introduce the magnifying glass to the children, explain what it is and how it is used
- Have each child hold the magnifying glass and look through it
- Walk around the garden area looking for bees and insects
- Concentrate on areas where there are flowers
- Talk about why bees can be found near flowers
- Whenever an insect is spotted allow the children to take turns looking through the magnifying glass

Evaluation: The children will enjoy looking through the magnifying glass. They will discover many different insects with excitement when they can see them magnified before them. The children should express themselves and in discussion new vocabulary should be used.

FLANNEL BOARD ACTIVITY

Curriculum Area: Language Arts

Objectives: Most children in this age group have minimal knowledge of other living things. It is important to increase their knowledge of animals and language skills. This activity will promote familiarity with new words and develop counting and matching skills.

Materials:

- Felt board (made of cardboard covered with white felt)
- Felt characters…using several different colours of felt create your own mother hen and as many baby chicks as there are children in your group
- Quiet reading area for activity

Procedure:

- Have children sit on floor in front of felt board
- Introduce the felt characters by placing them on the board where the children can see them
- Pass the felt characters around the circle so they can touch them and assign a chick to each child
- Allow each child to place their felt character on the felt board so that they may get the feeling of how felt sticks onto the felt board
- You will want to tell the children a story about the mother hen and her babies
- Using your imagination come up with a story that incorporates the mother hen, baby chicks, the colour of the chicks and counting to represent each one
- While you are telling the story have each child bring up the felt character that they have been given to hold in the order that it appears in the story
- Encourage them to listen to the story and prompt them to go up to the board to place their character as it is mentioned
- After the story is told talk about each character, ex. colour, how many and size

Evaluation: Involve the children in a story that holds their attention and makes them eager to participate. Safety precautions are important, so make sure the children do not put the pieces into their mouths. This is an activity that can help the children learn counting skills, colour recognition and will create an interest in farm animals ie: hens and chickens. The activity also centers around using their listening skills, turn taking and respect for others.

PLAY-DOH ACTIVITY

Curriculum Area: Language Arts / Sensory

Objectives: This activity will encourage creativity. You can use this experience as a follow-up to the Mother Hen story. It is important that children understand the concept that all living things reproduce. The activity will encourage participation and promotes skills in the areas of grouping and matching.

Materials:

- Child size table and chairs
- A variety of play-doh

Procedure:

- Have children sit around the table
- Have play-doh ready in the center of table
- Allow each child to choose the colour of their choice
- The children will be rolling out hen's eggs and worms
- Before they begin, give them some ideas of what you would like them to make. Show them an example
- Explain how hens lay eggs and baby chicks eat worms
- Be sure to walk around the table to assist each child

Evaluation: Praise each child's efforts. You may find that their concept of circle (representing egg shapes) and lines (representing worms) are still in the practicing stages. Constant hands-on assistance will be needed. You may want to use the play-doh again during the week to practice making shapes as a follow up activity.

FIVE GREEN FROGS

Curriculum Area: Language Arts

Objectives: Children enjoy finger plays. By using action songs, they have fun while developing new word skills and counting skills. This activity will promote group participation and foster good listening skills. The activity helps foster their ability to hold images of the words through song.

Materials:

- You will have to prepare for this activity by making or obtaining five simple green frog puppets
- Large group area
- 5 finger puppets made of green felt

Procedure:

- Have children sit in large circle
- Show them the finger puppets, allowing them to try them on if they wish
- Have the children sit quietly while you sing the song
- You may use any tune you wish changing the words to suit the frog theme. An example; sing the melody from three blind mice changing the words to: "5 green frogs, 5 green frogs, see how they hop, see how they hop."
- Repeat the song several times so that the children have a chance to become familiar with the verse
- Have the children raise their hands and use their fingers to imitate the actions that you are doing with the puppets
- If time allows let the children take turns using the finger puppets while everyone recites the verse

Evaluation: Most children love finger puppets. This activity encourages children to learn through song. The experience enhances their command of language and will improve listening and group interaction skills.

PAINTING ACTIVITY

Curriculum Area: Language Arts

Objectives: This activity will help strengthen children's creativity and fine motor skills. Another facet to this exercise is the development of classifying capabilities and the ability to hold an image.

Materials:

- Art centre
- Easel, paint, paper, and brushes

Procedure:

- Paint a large green frog on a piece of paper
- Hang the picture on an easel so that all the children can see it
- Have several colours of paint available
- Ask each child to choose a colour of paint that they would like to use and hand each child a brush
- Have them dip into the colour of their choice one at a time and go up to the easel putting a coloured speckle on the green frog
- When everyone has had a turn put all the names on the frog picture and hang it to dry

Evaluation: This is a very messy but fun exercise to do with the children. You definitely need a lot of hands on assistance. The concept of "speckles" also needs direction. You will probably be very impressed with the decision-making skills on the children's part to choose colours.

JUMP FROG JUMP

Curriculum Area: Gross Motor

Objectives: This activity is designed to develop large muscle control and recognition skills. The children will learn to respect others in taking turns. They will develop language skills and learn to interact in a positive way.

Materials:

- Large outdoor play area

Procedure:

- Demonstrate the action of crouching like a frog for the children
- Have the children imitate your action
- Have them jump up and down like a frog does making frog sounds "ribit, ribit"
- Start the game by having them get back into a crouched tuck position have them jump up only when their name is called
- Repeat until all the children's names have been called

Evaluation: You will find that the children's gross motor skills are limited at this developmental stage. The younger children may not be ready to master this skill. The children will try to mimic your action and should be praised for the attempt.

LET'S COLOUR YOUR PUPPY

Curriculum Area: Language Arts

Objectives: This activity will promote individual creativity. Each child will make their own choices on colour and style. They will increase their knowledge about animals while they develop their fine motor skills. The lesson will facilitate an ability to recreate a mental image. The children will practice sharing skills.

Materials:

- Art Centre
- Crayons
- Colouring picture of puppy (see attached – end of unit)
- Magazine or storybook pictures of puppies

Procedure:

- Have children sit around the table in groups of 3 or 4
- Encourage the other children to play at the other centres while they wait for their turn
- Set a colouring picture in front of each child
- Have the crayons available on the table for them to choose from
- Praise them as they begin to colour their picture
- Have pictures of dogs on the table for them to look at to get ideas
- When they are done, write their name on their picture and hang it on the wall
- Continue same procedure with next group

Evaluation: This is a great activity for the use of fine motor skills. You may want to try to encourage the children to use an appropriate colour crayon. Have them point at the pictures on the table and label the dog by name. Use the dog bone picture found in your unit as another colouring lesson.

FIND THE DOG BONE

Curriculum Area: Gross Motor

Objectives: The children will identify similarities between animal habits. They will develop their gross motor skills in an outdoor activity. They will observe and discover using classification skills.

Materials:

- Outdoor play area
- Tape
- Paper dog bones (see end of unit)

Procedure:

- Have the children form into a large group outdoors
- Tape the paper dog bones in various places throughout the playground
- Explain to the children that they are to walk around the yard looking for the dog bones (have one with you as a display for the children to look at before they start)
- Allow them time to walk around and discover the dog bones
- When all the bones have been found count all of them together to see how many bones were hiding

Evaluation: The children will undoubtedly be able to find most of the hidden dog bones. Some of the children were easily distracted toward the outdoor toys. Use a different picture and play again. This is an excellent exercise for developing gross motor skills.

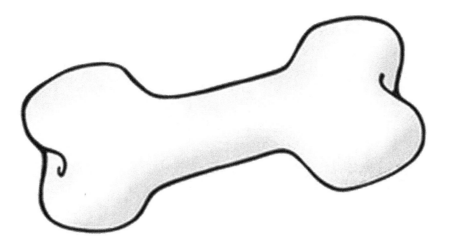

DO WE KNOW OUR SAFETY RULES?
SECTION II

SECTION II CONTENTS

SAFETY RHYME

Curriculum Area: Language Arts

Objectives: To encourage good safety habits. This activity will introduce streetlights and practice recognizing the colours red and green. We will actively explore using more than one of the senses. This exercise also encourages the awareness of safety and danger.

Materials:

- Large group area
- Safety Rhyme
- Large red Circles, large green circles

Procedures:

- Have children sit in front of you on the floor
- Introduce the colours red and green using large circles
- Recite the rhyme twice while the children listen:

> Red means stop
> Green means go
> Look both ways
> So you will know

- Hold up the coloured circles as they pertain to the story
- Have the children imitate the hand gestures with you, as you recite.
- e.g. turning head left and right hand up for stop with palm facing out arm extended for go

Evaluation: When the activity is done the children should start to have an awareness of the colours red and green and what they stand for. Encourage them to label the circles. All of the children will try to imitate the action however, the older children will be more successful.

COLOURING CIRCLES

Curriculum Area: Fine Motor / Creative

Objectives: This is a follow-up exercise to the safety rhyme. Encourage the identification of the colours red and green. The constant repetition of naming colours is a necessary component of learning. This activity will help the children to practice their cognitive skills in recognition and distinguishing. The exercise will promote good safety habits.

Materials:

- Table and chairs (child size)
- Paper Circles
- Red and Green crayons
- Straws

Procedures:

- Have children sit around the table in groups of two or three at a time
- Give them one circle and one red crayon each
- Ask them to colour the "stop light" red
- Have one red coloured circle in the middle of the table to demonstrate the completed activity
- Repeat the exercise with a green crayon
- Instruct them to colour the "go light" green
- When they have completed the activity attach the circles to the straws and stick them in the sand in the sandbox

Evaluation: Children love to use crayons. You will find that the concept of red and green is more easily understood than stop and go. If possible, this would be a good time to follow up the activity by taking them for a walk to see the streetlights.

RED LIGHT, GREEN LIGHT

Curriculum Area: Cognitive, gross motor

Objectives: This activity is done in the form of a game. It is a great follow-up activity to introducing the children to streetlights. There is a great use of gross motor skills. They experience team involvement, interaction and taking turns. We will also reinforce the concept of "stop and go".

Materials:

- Masking Tape
- Outdoor play area
- Coloured circles red and green to fit top of hand

Procedure:

- Have children form a line side by side
- Stand in front of them, far enough away so that they can run forward towards you
- Explain the rules of the game
- When you hold up the green light which will be a green circle taped to the top of your hand, the children are to run forward
- When you hold up the red circle which will be taped to your other hand the children are to stop
- Use an assistant to help you demonstrate the activity
- Repeat the activity several times to facilitate the learning of the colours red and green and stop and go

Evaluation: This is a fun activity for children. This game should be repeated for several days to help the children learn the concepts presented.

CIRCLE GAME

Curriculum Area: Gross motor / Sensory

Objectives: This activity follows the safety theme presented in this section. The children will all follow the same directions and become confident with the colours red and green. Language development, colours and shapes are reinforced. This activity promotes gross motor development.

Materials:

- Large open area
- Small red and green circles cut from coloured construction paper
- Masking tape

Procedure:

- Have the children form a large circle
- Tape one red circle on the top of each of their right hand
- Tape one green circle on the top of their left hand
- The teacher tapes a red and green circle on the top of his / her hand as well
- The tune for the song is sung to "hokey pokey"
- The teacher will demonstrate by singing a verse of the song while doing the actions
- Verse   "You put your red hand in"
               "You put your red hand out"
               "You put your red hand in and you shake it all about"
- Continue with activity repeating the verse using your green circle

Evaluation: Most of the children will try to imitate the Teacher's actions. You may find that some of the younger children will need assistance. Try the song verse using other colours as well. This activity will help the children develop a sense of direction and word recognition as well.

A WALK THROUGH CITY STREETS

Curriculum Area: Social Studies

Objectives: This activity will bring the concept of "red light, green light" to reality. The children will also see many different people on the streets in their community. The children will use their cognitive ability relating the coloured circles with the streetlights.

Materials:

- Outdoors to an area where there are street lights
- Coloured circles
- One red coloured circle
- One green coloured circle

Procedure:

- Explain to the children that they are going for a walk and that they will see streetlights. A picture of street lights would be a great visual aid at this time
- Go to the nearest set of lights
- When the light turns red point to it and have the children label by saying stop
- Show them the red circle that they have been using in their activities
- Wait for the light to change and repeat the activity using the green circle
- Cross the intersection to reinforce to them that green signifies "go"

Evaluation: You have given the children a "safety" experience. They have used gross motor skills, language skills and classification. Their perception and cognitive development is at a stage where they may have only recognized the colour change and not the actual concept. This activity should be repeated several times as they develop.

STOOD UP DANGEROUSLY

Curriculum Area: Language Arts

Objectives: Following our safety theme, we will introduce the danger of standing on inappropriate objects or climbing in areas that are dangerous. We will promote safety rules using a stuffed animal to promote the concept that animals can get hurt too. This activity will facilitate the use of language skills, promote listening skills and demonstrate the feeling of empathy for others.

Materials:

- Reading Area
- Band-Aids
- Stuffed Bear

Procedure:

- Have children sit in a circle
- Introduce the bear
- Explain to the children that bear must always be careful so that he doesn't get hurt
- Recite the rhyme with actions (twice)

  Silly little teddy bear
  Stood up on a rocking chair (make rocking movement)
  Now he has to stay in bed (lay hands on head)
  With a bandage round his head

- Give each child a Band-Aid
- Have each child take their turn putting a Band-Aid on the bear and comforting him

Evaluation: The use of a stuffed animal and the Band-Aids will keep the children's attention. Each child will show emotion in his or her own way. Walk around the room bringing attention to areas that would be dangerous to climb up on. Emphasize positive procedures.

BRUISES AND BANDAGES

Curriculum Area: Dramatic Play / Social

Objectives: Children enjoy cuddling and nurturing. Using a doll or a stuffed animal, the children will experience the ability to express their feelings, identify body parts and interact in symbolic play. Fine motor development is used in grasping and manipulating the Band-Aids.

Materials:

- Band-Aids
- Dolls or stuffed animals
- Dramatic play centre

Procedure:

- Have children choose either a doll or a stuffed animal
- Educator chooses one too
- Have the students walk their doll on a chair
- At the same time the Educator also goes through the motions with his/her doll
- Have your doll slip off the chair, cuddle the doll and tell her she must never stand on chairs because it is dangerous
- Put a Band-Aid on the doll's knee
- Have the children imitate your actions
- Hand a Band-Aid to each child and assist them in applying it to the wounded area of their doll
- Have them try to verbalize the word "danger" to their doll

Evaluation: This activity involves the use of many developmental areas. You can have a discussion about dangerous areas. The day after the activity is done have them remove the Band-Aids and tell their dolls "all better".

TAKING BABIES FOR A WALK

Curriculum Area: Gross Motor / Social Studies

Objectives: This activity will help children to develop a sense of belonging. The concept of responsibility is introduced with the understanding of taking care of someone else. Gross motor skills are used throughout this activity.

Materials:

- Dolls
- Toy Strollers
- Stuffed Animals
- Outdoor Play Area

Procedure:

- Have the children use strollers or carry their babies depending on the number of toy strollers available
- Explain the activity to the children; They are going outside for a walk with their babies
- The educator will take his / her doll out for a walk also
- Have the children walk around the outdoor play area pushing their babies in the strollers
- Stop periodically and have the children sit their babies on the bench and have a break

Evaluation: Children enjoy role-playing. They will demonstrate empathy towards their dolls or stuffed animals. This activity should be short in length. Allow the children to socialize with each other and to enjoy the sharing concept.

DANGER HAND DISPLAY

Curriculum Area: Language Arts

Objectives: Children of this age group are unaware of danger unless safety and the dangers involved are emphasized to them. This activity promotes awareness of danger in a child's world. The exercise facilitates word recognition and develops a sense of curiosity in the child.

Materials:

- Large group reading area
- Danger hand cut outs (see sample at end of this unit)

Procedure:

- Have children sit in a circle on the floor
- Introduce your danger hand cut out to the children
- Explain to them the action of hand up with palm facing out means "danger"
- Have the children imitate your action and repeat the word "danger"
- Recite 2 or 3 different safety rules that will help them stay safe
- Ex: "do not stand on chairs, do not climb on top of cupboards, stay away from the stove"
- Take children to areas in the daycare that you can put your "danger hand" sticker on to reinforce the concept of safety

Evaluation: This activity is somewhat advanced. You may want to repeat this activity for several days to allow time and repetition to help the younger toddlers understand the concept. As you see the children develop an understanding for the danger concept use some new "danger areas" to reinforce proper safety.

FIND THE DANGER HANDS

Curriculum Area: Cognitive / Gross Motor

Objectives: This activity develops perception skills. The children will learn to search for a particular object and be able to identify it. Language will also be practiced. Labeling and the use of gross motor skills will also be introduced.

Materials:

- Large play area in kitchen centre (kitchen and bathroom)
- Cut outs of danger hand
- Tape

Procedure:

- Place danger hands around the room where danger could occur
- Explain activity to the children
- They will go into areas of the centre looking for danger hands
- When a child finds a sign they point to the sign and say "danger"
- Go to each object that is discovered and explain to the children what the danger would be
- Continue until all the hands are found and safety rules have been explained to them
- Allow the children to hold up their hands towards the objects and try to get them to repeat the word danger

Evaluation: The children enjoy gross motor activities. When you explain a situation that could be dangerous. You must keep the explanation short, clear and concise in order to keep their attention. This activity can be repeated several times throughout the year. Use the danger hands in your outdoor area as well.

STEP UP

Curriculum Area: Gross Motor

Objectives: This activity is designed to facilitate the development of gross motor skills. Since many gross motor skills are limited at this age, the exercise promotes the practice skills needed in order to develop, increase balance and coordination. The activity also encourages the child to build self-confidence.

Materials:

- A play apparatus in the outdoor play area
- Hard cover books of various sizes

Procedure:

- Place a book onto the floor and encourage the child to step up onto it.
- Hold the child's hand for support (if needed)
- Change the size of the book as the child's balance increases
- Once the children have mastered the skill of stepping up take them to an outdoor play apparatus that has stairs and have them practice walking up

Evaluation: The older toddlers will master this skill quicker than the younger children. You may find that some of the children will be reluctant to try this skill without first holding the hand of an assistant for support. Most, if not all, of the children will use the handrail when stepping up. This skill should be practiced regularly.

MAKING WATER WINGS

Curriculum Area: Language Arts

Objectives: This activity should follow the "swimming pool" activity. Safety is a prime concern when children are near water. Water wings are important for the child's safety. The activity promotes language development and develops creativity.

Materials:

- Child size table and chairs
- Orange construction paper
- Glue
- Scissors
- Measuring tape

Procedure:

- Do this activity with two children at a time
- Have them sit at the table
- Show the child a finished water wing as a model of what they are going to do
- Using a measuring tape, measure each child's arm size
- Using hand over hand, cut the orange paper into strips
- Use masking tape or glue to fasten wings to child's arm
- Repeat activity until all children have their own set marking each pair with their names
- Sing summer songs while creating

Evaluation: Most young children have worn water wings so that they are familiar with them. At this age group most children will need hand over hand assistance with cutting. When doing any of the summer activities have the children wear their water wings.

SWIMMING POOL

Curriculum Area: Dramatic Play / Language Arts

Objectives: When enjoying summer activities, the focus must be on good safety habits. This activity will promote language development, strengthen gross motor skills and facilitate socialization skills.

Materials:

- Large play area (depending on weather. The outdoors would be most appropriate)
- Large blue blanket
- Construction paper water wings

Procedure:

- Have children sit on floor in a circle and explain the activity to them
- Put each child's water wings on them
- Spread the blanket out in the open area
- Put your water wings on and have the children stand with you on the blanket
- Explain to the children that the blue blanket is going to represent water. We will call it the "pretend swimming pool"
- Sing the "Swimming Pool" song demonstrating the actions
  Swimming, swimming in my swimming pool
  When days are hot, when days are cool
  In my swimming pool"
- Have the children lay on their tummies and move their arms to pretend they are swimming
- Demonstrate different swimming strokes such as breast strokes, back strokes etc.
- Repeat activity until children start to lose interest

Evaluation: This activity follows up on the previous activities about swimming. Some of the children may have never swum in a pool or large body of water. In this case pictures of children swimming would be useful. It is important to talk to the children about why wearing water wings is so important when they are near water. You will find that most of the children will enjoy this exercise because of the gross motor movement.

SUMMER ENVIRONMENT
SECTION III

SECTION III CONTENTS

SUMMER ACTIVITIES

Curriculum Area: Language Arts

Objectives: This activity will introduce the children to summer activities. Most children love the summer fun outdoors. The repetition of summer words will enhance language development. The activity will promote interest and curiosity. The children will learn to label objects and relate to objects that they see in pictures.

Materials:

- Large open reading area
- Pictures of outdoor play (cut from magazines)

Procedure:

- Have children sit together in circle
- Talk about some of the activities that you can do in the summer
- Show them one picture at a time
- Explain what is happening in the picture
- Ask them questions about what each picture represents
- Allow each child to touch each picture
- Pass the picture around the circle for a close up look

Evaluation: Most of the children will respond to the pictures. You will note that the discussion will be one-sided as their language development is still in its practicing stages. Use words to promote language development such as "swimming" and "swing". When the activity is complete put the pictures on a wall so that the children can look at them.

COLOUR A FLOWER

Curriculum Area: Creative / Language Arts

Objectives: This activity will introduce the children to different types of flowers. The children will use their creativity and the use of their fine motor skills. By repeating the word flower they practice their use of language.

Materials:

- Art area
- Small table and chairs
- Photo copy drawing of flower
- Crayons

Procedure:

- Activity should be done with no more than three children at a time
- When the children are seated around the table show them the picture that they will be colouring
- Pass out a copy of the picture to each child
- Spread the coloured crayons in the middle of the table so that they may choose the colours that they want to use
- Praise them for their creativity as they colour
- Help those who need assistance holding the crayon (using pincer grip)
- Sign each child's name on their picture when they are done and have each child help you hang their flower on the wall

Evaluation: Children are very eager to use crayons. They will probably scribble on their pages, some changing colours, others using the same crayon. Do many colouring activities to increase the proficiency of their fine motor skills.

A BOUQUET OF FLOWERS

Curriculum Area: Language Arts / Science

Objectives: Children enjoy looking at objects that are bright in colour. Introducing flowers to children helps them learn to distinguish one flower from another, appreciate beauty and use classification.

Materials:

- Outdoor Area
- Circle area for reading
- Artificial flowers

Procedure:

- If weather permits take the children outside, if not have them sit in a circle in the reading area
- Show them the bouquet of artificial flowers
- Talk about the different colours of the flowers
- Allow each child to choose a flower from the bouquet to hold in their hand
- Put the remaining flowers on the floor in front of them
- Give each child a plastic container (ice cream size) to use as a vase
- Have the children choose flowers and place them in their vase to make an arrangement
- When the activity is completed take the children outside to a garden to look at the flowers

Evaluation: Since children are still in the sensory learning stage, some may put the flowers in the vase while others will touch the flowers or possibly put them in their mouths. To help the children learn to appreciate nice things, leave the flowers out for the week. You also may want to show them pictures of flowers and point them out in an illustration when reading a story.

FRUITS WE EAT IN THE SUMMER

Curriculum Area: Social Studies / Language

Objectives: This activity promotes language skills. Most toddlers may not necessarily know the name of the fruit they are eating. By using word repetition the children become familiar with the names of fruits. Colour recognition is also part of this activity.

Materials:

- Reading Area
- A book illustrating pictures of different fruits

Procedure:

- Have children sit on floor in reading area
- Introduce the book
- Repeat the word "fruit"
- Read the book stopping at each page to show children illustrations
- After saying the name of a fruit and its colour have the children repeat the words to you
- When completed, go back over each picture saying the name of the fruit and the colour representation

Evaluation: The children will recognize some of the fruit. They will try to repeat the names of the more common ones. When the children are having a fruit snack repeat the name of the fruit snack with them.

PAINTING WITH FRUIT

Curriculum Area: Language / Art Creativity

Objectives: Most children love to create using paints. This activity promotes children's individual creativity and allows them to make choices in choosing colour and design. The exercise facilitates the use of fine motor skills.

Materials:

- Small table and chairs
- Several different colours of paint
- Fresh peach halves
- Paper
- Paint Snacks
- Plastic containers (margarine tub size)

Procedure:

- Do the activity alternating with 2 or 3 children at a time
- Give each child seated at the table a piece of paper
- Put paint trays in the middle of the table ensuring easy access for each child
- Give each child ½ of a freshly cut peach
- Demonstrate by dipping the cut side of the fruit into the paint and then pressing it firmly onto the paper (a stamp effect)
- Continue activity until each child has made at least 3 imprints on their sheet

Evaluation: Children enjoy the hands-on experience working with paint. The novelty of using fruit as a tool to make a design will encourage the child's interest. This activity will reinforce their recognition of different fruit.

TOSS AND CATCH

Curriculum Area: Gross Motor

Objectives: It is very important to continually increase the development of gross motor skills. This activity will develop eye-hand co-ordination and increase the skill of catching a rolling ball.

Materials:

- Outdoor area (if weather permits)
- Large open indoor area
- Beach ball

Procedure:

- Have the children sit in a large circle with their legs spread in a "V" position
- Sit with them and roll the beach ball to each child
- Have each child roll it back to you
- Be sure that each child has several turns

Evaluation: The skill involved in this game may be advanced for some of the younger Toddlers' development stage. However using an assistant to help them will allow them to participate in the game. Repeat this activity often when gross motor development is focused.

SEASHELLS

Curriculum Area: Language Arts

Objectives: This activity enables the children to experience curiosity and interest in other surroundings. Word repetition facilitates language development. Sensory development is also involved in the activity when seashells are passed around to the children to feel the texture.

Materials:

- Reading area
- Seashells

Procedure:

- Have children sit in a group in reading area
- Introduce the seashells to them
- Allow them time to touch the seashells to feel the texture
- Take five seashells and lay them on the floor in front of you
- Choose seashells that are different in size
- Show picture of places that you would find seashells (ex: ocean or a beach)

Evaluation: The children should enjoy touching the seashells. This activity is a great learning experience for children who live in areas where seashells are not a common environmental object.

SHELL COLLECTING

Curriculum Area: Social Studies / Science

Objectives: Most children find enjoyment in playing in the sandbox. This activity is centered around the sandbox. By allowing the children to put the shells in the sandbox you are enabling them to be able to identify the concept that seashells are found in the sand.

Materials:

- Sandbox
- Seashells
- Plastic shovels

Procedure:

- Depending on the weather, this activity can be done indoors or outdoors
- Give each child 2 seashells and a plastic shovel
- Have all the children go to the sandbox area
- Through demonstration show the children how to use the shovel to hide the seashells
- Have the children bury their shells in the sand and then dig them up again

Evaluation: You may find that the children may be reluctant at first to hide their shells in the sand. After several demonstrations they will probably start to imitate your behavior. You can also do this activity putting the seashells in a bucket.

BLOWING BUBBLES

Curriculum Area: Fine Motor / Science

Objectives: Fine motor skills and hand-eye coordination is an intricate part in the physical development of children. Having children blow bubbles helps build muscle control using the mouth to blow bubbles. This exercise introduces Toddlers to the abstract context that not all things are what they seem. The bubble looks like a ball floating in the sky, then it "pops" and it is gone.

Materials:

- Bubble soap
- Bubble blowing stick

Procedure:

- This exercise should be done outdoors
- Show the children the bubble set
- Demonstrate by blowing a bubble and pointing to it floating in the air
- Have each child take a turn blowing a bubble and watching it float upward
- Hold the bubble stick for the children when they blow their bubble
- On the second turn have each child hold their own bubble stick while turn taking

Evaluation: Children will be fascinated watching the bubbles float upward. They may have trouble blowing their own bubbles because they are in the developmental stage of facial muscle control. Re-do the activity practicing facial muscle control.

SUMMER SEASON

Curriculum Area: Literature

Objectives: This activity introduces the season of summer and helps the children recognize the season by name. Reading a story with a summer theme enhances language skills and shows them the characteristics of the season of summer.

Materials:

- Library quiet reading area
- Storybook with summer theme (camping)

Procedure:

- Children will sit together on the floor in quiet area (cozy corner)
- Introduce the book cover to them
- Talk about going camping and staying in a tent
- Read the storybook to the children, stopping at each page to show them the illustrations

Evaluation: Children at Toddler age have short attention spans. You may find that some of the children will be more attentive than others. Use voice inflections to help hold their interest.

HOT AND COLD

Curriculum Area: Science / Sensory

Objectives: This activity will differentiate hot from cold and also help the children identify the two temperatures with the change of seasons. We will associate summer with warm temperatures and winter with cold temperatures. They will use their senses (visual sensory). The children will develop language skills with the new words used.

Materials:

- Large area for circle
- Ice cubes
- Bowls
- Heating pad

Procedure:

- Have the children sit on the floor in a circle
- Talk about warm days in summer and cold days in winter
- Put ice cubes in a bowl and put the bowl on the floor in the middle of the circle
- Preheat the heating pad before the activity begins
- Unplug the heating pad and put it in the middle of the circle
- Tell the children it is warm in the summer and have them put their hand on the heating pad to feel the "warm" temperature
- Do the some using the bowl of ice cubes to demonstrate the temperature in winter

Evaluation: The children will enjoy this activity using their sense of touch to feel the sensation of hot and cold.

BAREFOOT ACTIVITY

Curriculum Area: Gross Motor / Sensory

Objectives: In order for the children to understand texture they must be able to feel it. In this activity the children will learn about different surface textures. Smooth, rough, soft and hard textures will be introduced.

Materials:

- Outdoor area
- Different surfaces to walk on

Procedure:

- Take the children to the play area outdoors
- Allow the children to remove their shoes and socks
- Make sure the surfaces are free of any debris and sharp objects
- Have them walk in the grass
- Have them step on cement
- Walk on a black rubber outdoor mat
- Step in the dirt
- Step on a smooth board
- Ask the children which surface is cooler, harder, warmer, softer, rough or smooth
- After the activity is done have the children wash their feet in a pail with soapy water

Evaluation: Most children enjoy being barefoot. Allow them to make their barefoot prints on the surfaces. Have the children use their hands to touch the surfaces that they investigated barefoot. You can repeat the same questions.

WATER TABLE

Curriculum Area: Language Arts

Objectives: The children will enhance their language skills through hands on play with toys, repeating words such as water and boat. Eye-hand coordination and gross motor skills are a focal point of this exercise. You may incorporate multi-cultural learning by using pictures of boats used in different countries.

Materials:

- Children's water table
- Plastic boats
- Pictures of boats (variety)

Procedure:

- Two to three children gather around the water table
- Show them the pictures of different boats
- Hand each child a boat and tell them they are going to sail their boats in the water
- Allow the children to submerge their boats in the water
- While playing make noises "rrr" imitating the sound a motor would make
- Repeat words such as boat, water, summer and have the children repeat them with you

Evaluation: Most of the children enjoy playing at the water table. You may find some of the children reluctant to play in the water at all. If so, allow them to have another activity. Display the pictures of the boats on a board so that the children can look at them throughout the day.

COLOURS AND SHAPES
SECTION IV

SECTION IV CONTENTS

COLOURS AND SHAPES

Curriculum Area: Literature

Objectives: This activity will introduce the children to colours and shapes. The activity will enable children to recognize a circle and a square of two different colours: red and green. Language development is an essential part of this activity.

Materials:

- Reading centre
- Book – pre-school literature colours and shapes (choose from many common pre-school books on colours and shapes)

Procedure:

- Have the children gather in a circle on the floor in front of you in the reading area
- Tell them you are going to read them a story, showing them the illustration on the cover
- While reading the book, stop on each page to show the children the pictures
- Repeat the word labels for the children and shapes as often as their attention allows

Evaluation: The children will recognize some of the basic shapes and colours. Assistance may be needed for some of the younger children. Try to focus on the colours red and green.

COLOURING ACTIVITY

Curriculum Area: Creative Arts

Objectives: Children are interested in participating in hands-on activities. This activity will introduce them to shapes and colours. By participating in this exercise, the children will develop an understanding of differences between objects and colours. They will develop creativity, language and fine motor skills.

Materials:

- Small size table and chairs
- Paper, crayons and tape

Procedure:

- Start the activity with 2 or 3 children at a time
- Have the children sit around the table at the art centre
- Pass out a piece of paper with a circle shape and a square shape drawn on it to each child
- Put the crayons in the centre of the table and allow each child to choose the crayon of their choice
- Encourage them to say the word that represents the colour they have chosen
- Encourage them to change the colour of the crayon for each different shape that they colour
- When they are done write their names on their drawing

Evaluation: It is important to encourage children to learn the shapes and colours of objects so that they start to recognize them. Although it is an abstract concept, you will find that through this exercise the children will start to recognize other objects by shape or colour. You will find that most of the children will not recognize the shapes at first and will colour in a scribbling motion.

THE COLOURS IN OUR ENVIRONMENT

Curriculum Area: Social Studies

Objectives: Identifying objects in our out-door environment allows the children to develop colour recognition and to be able to use words to describe colour. This is a gross motor activity, also encouraging them to use their eyes to view the world around them.

Materials:

- Outdoor area
- Play equipment, flowers and all outdoor surroundings

Procedure:

- Take the children outdoors
- Point to different objects and say the name of the colour out loud
- Have the children repeat the word
- Do this activity with several different objects
- Ask the children to point at objects that are red etc.
- Repeat the procedure using different colours

Evaluation: Moving from one activity to another keeps the children's attention. You will find that several of them will repeat the colour words. You may also find that some of them will identify the object by saying the name as well. Repeat this activity in another outdoor surrounding.

THE COLOUR OF FRUIT

Curriculum Area: Language Arts

Objectives: This activity follows the shapes and colours theme. Since children need to develop skills in recognition by word we will look at identifying several different fruit using word and colour recognition. We also want to introduce the children to many different fruit that they may not be familiar with. The exercise will develop language skills and verbalization.

Materials:

- Reading Centre
- Picture book showing fruit

Procedure:

- Have the children sit in the reading area
- Show them the picture on the cover of the book
- Go through the picture book [page by page concentrating on the colour of the fruit
- Have the children repeat the word after you
- When completed, go through the pictures of the common fruits and repeat the words

Evaluation: The children are likely to be aware of several of the fruit. Practicing colour through introduction to fruit allows children to repeat their colour recognition and also to become aware of the different fruit we have to eat. We use labeling by pointing to objects and naming them by colour and word recognition.

PREPARING FRUIT

Curriculum Area: Social Studies / Language Arts

Objectives: In this activity we will continue to develop language skills, classification skills and colour recognition. We will display several different types of fruit using organizational skills to identify colour and shape. Fine motor skills are also practiced by having each child take turns cleaning the fruit.

Materials:

- Kitchen eating area
- Bowls, fruit and water
- Share paring knife (to be used by Educator)

Procedure:

- Have the children sit around the lunch table
- The Educator will give each child a fruit
- Put a bucket of warm water on the table
- Each child will wash his / her piece of fruit and have the children repeat the word
- The Educator will say the name for the shape of the fruit and have the children repeat the word
- The Educator will then cut and peel each piece of fruit
- The children will then place the pieces of cut fruit into the appropriate bowls

Evaluation: The children will enjoy the exercise but you will see that they will be anxious to eat the fruit. They will repeat most of the words developing language skills. The more often you repeat this type of exercise the more the children will be able to distinguish colours and fruits. This is an ideal activity using vegetables as well.

LET'S HAVE A PICNIC

Curriculum Area: Social Science / Science

Objectives: Children love to be outdoors and love to snack. We will incorporate both by having an outdoor picnic. We will invite people of different ages to join in the fun. This activity will help to develop socialization skills and language through words. A key focus is learning to share together.

Materials:

- Grassy Outdoor area
- Blanket
- Picnic basket of fruit

Procedure:

- Explain to the children that they will be going on a picnic
- Show then the picnic basket with the fruit inside
- Take them outside and find a grassy area to lay the blanket down
- Spread the blanket out and have the children sit down on it
- Put the basket in the middle of the blanket and share the fruit between all the children and any adults that are present
- Allow the children to play with each other and enjoy the experience

Evaluation: Most of the children will love the picnic experience outdoors. It is important to build social skills between the children. This is a great activity for socialization.

RED IS BEST

Curriculum Area: Literature

Objectives: To show the children that many different objects can be the colour red. We enhance language skills by reviewing the pronunciation of the word red using a story about the colour red or pictures of objects that are red. Another objective of the activity is to develop good listening skills.

Materials:

- Cozy corner reading area
- Choose pictures from magazines that are red in colour
- Choose any common pre-school storybook that describes the colour red

Procedure:

- Have the children sit in front of you in your reading area
- Show them the cover of the book if you choose to read the story
- If using magazines, show them the pictures one at a time saying the name of the object using red to describe the colour
- When you have finished the lesson show the illustrations again repeating the words

Evaluation: You will find that some of the younger children will have a much shorter attention span and may not stay focused for the entire activity. Have the older children point to something in the room that is red. You may also want to use this activity with other colours.

STACKING GAME

Curriculum Area: Fine Motor / Science

Objectives: This activity will continue to reinforce the theme of colours and shapes. Using blocks, the children will develop fine motor skills, hand to eye coordination and colour and shape recognition. This activity will build the children's curiosity about simple science and mechanics – how to stack blocks without toppling them. Language will also be practiced.

Materials:

- Block play area
- Red and Blue blocks

Procedure:

- Have two children do this activity at a time
- Give one child the blue blocks and the other the red blocks
- Demonstrate how to build a five story high tower
- Show them the block and tell them that it is a square
- Have them repeat the word square
- Repeat the same activity using the colour words
- When they have completed or tried to complete the task of building a tower allow them some free play and have the next two children engage in the activity

Evaluation: Most of the children will enjoy this game. You will notice that some of the children will have more advanced eye hand coordination than others. Repeat this activity throughout the development stages using different coloured blocks.

HAT SORTING GAME

Curriculum Area: Social Studies

Objectives: To teach children about colours and shapes, we will use objectives that they are familiar with. We will also introduce multiculturalism by showing the children hats worn by different ethnic groups. The development of sorting skills, classifying skills and language will also be enhanced through this activity.

Materials:

- Large area for group activity
- Several hats of different size, shape, colour and origin

Procedure:

- Explain to the children that they are going to play a game using Hats
- Have them sit on the floor in a big circle
- Put all the hats in the middle of the circle
- Pick up each hat and explain the colour and the shape
- Ask each child to go and get a hat, each one being different, Example: "Jeremy please go and get the blue ball hat" etc.
- Guide the child to the proper hat
- When they all have a hat, have them put them back in the middle of the circle directing them to put the hats in a specific area

Evaluation: Most of the children will want to put the hats on their heads. Allow them to do so for fun. The children can help in the sorting of the hats, which teaches them to be able to group, label and classify. This is a great activity to do using shoes as well.

A MATCHING GAME

Curriculum Area: Language Arts/Cognitive

Objectives: This activity will introduce new colours. Children must learn to be able to recognize different colours. This exercise will enhance that skill. New colours will also develop language as the children try to repeat new words.

Materials:

- Quiet area for puzzle play
- Puzzle board game (hand crafted using a piece of bristle board draw different shapes on the board that connect together) use a different colour for each shape
- Laminate your puzzle board if possible
- Using heavy paper, trace the playing board then cut out all the shapes
- Colour all the cut-outs to match those on the board

Procedure:

- Have one child play the with the game at a time. Some assistance will be needed
- Introduce the board game
- Point out all the different colours and shapes
- Demonstrate how to play the game board by matching the pieces on the board
- When one child has completed the game, have the next child play
- Continue until all the children have had a turn

Evaluation: The children enjoy holding the coloured pieces in their hands. Some will put the proper pieces on top of the match on the game board. Use this game often as part of the colours curriculum.

Debra Franceschini

CIRCLE LEAP FROG

Curriculum Area: Gross Motor

Objectives: This activity is designed to further develop children's gross motor skills. They will be able to recognize certain colours while following direction and using their listening skills.

Materials:

- Eight large differently coloured circles, about a foot in diameter
- Large outdoor play area

Procedures:

- Take the children outdoors
- Find a suitable area free of equipment to play the game
- Place the eight coloured circles on the ground
- Space them out, evenly apart so that the toddlers have to jump slightly to step on them
- Instruct the children to follow in a line
- They are to step on each coloured circle and then go to the back of the line to wait for their turn again
- As the children play leaping from one coloured circle to the next ask them one at a time "What colour are you jumping on?"

Evaluation: Children love to run and play. All of the children will try to walk or jump   on the circles at least once. Use the coloured circles again to play another jumping game, this time have the children sit on the circles.

MAKING COLOURS

Curriculum Area: Science

Objectives: The making of colours project will creat an awareness of making things change appearance. By mixing two colours together the children will create a new colour. They will use fine motor skills as well as develop language skills using words. We will introduce the concept of change.

Materials:

- Art centre
- Small art table
- Red paint, blue paint
- Paint brushes
- Art paper

Procedure:

- Do this activity with two or three children at a time
- Have them sit around the table
- Put a container of blue paint and red paint on the table
- Put out an empty container as well
- Using the paints on the table mix two colours together to show them the colour purple
- Give each child a paint brush and a piece of paper
- Have each child dip their brush in the mixed paint and make strokes using the colour purple on their paper

Evaluation: Hands-on experience is always a good learning tool for children. The children enjoy mixing paint together. Colours that are not primary are often hard for young children to identify. This activity helps them recognize new colours. You may want to repeat this activity several times using other colours, for example using red and yellow to make orange.

FOLLOW THE FOOTPRINTS

Curriculum Area: Gross Motor/Language

Objectives: This activity will again reinforce colour and shape recognition. Gross motor skills will be used focusing on large muscle co-ordination. The children will also be introduced to the concept of symbols being used to identify colours.

Materials:

- Large outdoor open space
- Large coloured footprint shapes

Procedure:

- Take the children outdoors
- Find a suitable area, free of play equipment, to play the game
- Place the coloured footprints on the ground
- Space them in a moving forward direction as if you were walking   forward
- Ask the children to form a line
- Explain to them through demonstration to walk on each foot one at a time in a natural fashion
- Say the colour of each footprint as you stand on it
- Have the children say the name of as many of the colours as they can
- Continue the game in an orderly fashion until the children have had two or three turns each

Evaluation: There is no sequence to this activity. They will enjoy walking on the prints but may not do so in any particular order. Place the footprints sideways and have the children practice walking sideways.

I'M SPECIAL
SECTION V

SECTION V CONTENTS

PICTURES OF CHILDREN

Curriculum Area: Language Arts

Objectives: At this stage of growth children start to develop a sense of autonomy. This activity will teach the children about themselves and how they may be different from others. Children will often relate well to pictures of other children. Developmental skills such as eye-hand co-ordination, classifying, sorting and facilitating of literacy will be visited.

Materials:

- Pictures of children (include all ethnic groups)
- Child size table and chair
- Large group area

Procedure:

- Have the children sit on the floor in a circle
- Sit on a chair and explain to them that you will be showing them some pictures of other children like them
- Explain the pictures by pointing out the characteristics ex. "The little girl in the picture has blonde hair just like you"
- After the children have seen all of the pictures, have them break into small groups, three or four at a table
- Set the pictures on the table and have each child point to the one that they think looks most like them
- Compare brown eyes, blue eyes and dark or light colour hair regardless of ethnicity

Evaluation: It is very interesting to notice how young children have no bias as to race or colour. You may ask them to choose a picture that most resembles them. If an African American has the closest resemblance (for example similar hair colour, eye colour) that will be the picture that the child will pick even though he or she is Caucasian. They will learn that everyone has different characteristics. They will choose similarities and differences.

APPEARANCE ACTIVITY

Curriculum Area: Science/Sensory

Objectives: It is important to teach children that every person has a difference in appearance and that appearances change over time as well. We will introduce the concept of "before" and "after" in this lesson. The activity will also describe the concept of change as related to how our bodies change as we grow. Many senses will be explored such as touch, sight, smell and taste. We will use comparisons and encourage children to observe detail.

Materials:

- Large bowl, Jell-O crystals, spoons and small plastic bowls
- Kettle
- Kitchen area

Procedure:

- Have the children sit around a table in the kitchen area
- Show them the Jell-O while it is still in crystal form
- Put a small amount in a bowl and let each child feel the texture
- Heat the water in the kettle remembering to follow all safety rules with the children
- Explain each step of preparation as you prepare using hot and cold water to mix ingredients
- When water is poured into Jell-O crystals allow each child a short turn stirring the Jell-O
- Using a ladle pour enough Jell-O in bowls for each child to have a serving
- Bring the children back in a few hours when the Jell-O is set
- Allow each child to touch the Jell-O to feel the texture before tasting

Evaluation: This is an observing activity. The children will watch the jell-O transform from liquid to a firm texture. This helps introduce them to the concept of change. You may also accomplish the same goal by using pudding or freezing ice cubes.

TEN LITTLE FINGERS

Curriculum Area: Language Arts/Fine Motor

Objectives: This activity will bring awareness to the children of their physical characteristics. Most children at the toddler stage of development would be unaware that they have ten fingers or toes. We will also focus on the fact that some children are extra special and may be unique in a different way. We will develop language and fine motor skills through finger play rhymes.

Materials:

- Reading area
- Finger play using ten fingers (you can use finger puppets and tell them a story – be creative for example, sing ten little Indians or play this little piggy went to the market)

Procedure:

- Have the children sit on the floor in front of you
- Show them your fingers and count them out loud
- Have the children show you their ten fingers
- Count each child's fingers individually
- Act out the finger play two times
- Go slowly so that the children can start to imitate the actions
- When the finger play is complete, talk about the different characteristics of the children's fingers

Evaluation: Some of the children will be able to count a few of their fingers out loud on their own. Repetition is the key to success in this activity. Discuss with the children other things that fingers and toes do (for example, hold objects, make clapping sounds etc)

RHYMES WITH MOVEMENT

Curriculum Area: Gross Motor /Language

Objectives: Children do not generally focus on why body parts move. This activity will give each child the opportunity to be in tune with his/her own body movement. The exercise will help to develop gross motor skills and coordination. We will enhance language skills using word such as head and neck.

Materials:

- Large area for group activity

Procedure:

- Have the children stand in a circle in the open area
- Using the theme melody from "The Hokey Pokey" explain to the children what they are going to do
- Show them the actions as you sing the words "lift your head up high, put your head down low"
- Repeat the words and actions several times allowing the children time to catch on to the actions
- Praise them for trying to perform the actions

Evaluation: Since the movements to the action song are quite simple the children will be able to imitate the actions fairly well. Repeat the rhyme another day as an outdoor activity.

HAND PRINTS, THUMB PRINTS

Curriculum Area: Science/Fine Motor

Objectives: Everyone has a unique hand and thumb print. In this activity we will let the children do something that they love to do, put paint all over their hands! Using their creativity they will discover their individual hand and thumb print and then compare with others. They will use fine motor sensory when they feel the paint on their hands.

Materials:

- Art Centre
- Table and Chairs
- Paint, paper and tinfoil pans

Procedure:

- This activity is best done with two children at a time
- Have the paint and paper ready before the activity begins
- When the children are seated put a piece of paper in front of them
- Have the children lay their hands flat in a tinfoil pan of paint
- Using hand over hand have them take their hand and press it firmly on the paper, making an imprint
- Take their thumb and dip it into the paint
- Make a thumb print on the paper
- You can make several thumbprints and use them as a design around the hand print
- Compare the children's handprints and explain the differences to the child

Evaluation: This will be quite a messy experience! The children will thoroughly enjoy this activity. Try this exercise using feet and toes.

FOOTPRINTS IN THE SAND

Curriculum Area: Science/Gross Motor

Objectives: This activity will familiarize children with their own body parts. Make them aware that footprints come in all shapes and sizes. The exercise will develop gross motor skills and language development. Hopefully, at the end of this activity the children will be able to recognize their own footprint.

Materials:

- Outdoor sandbox
- Bare feet

Procedure:

- Take the children outdoors to the sandbox
- Have them remove their shoes and socks
- Have two or three children press their footprint into the sand
- Have all of the children do the activity
- Line the prints up in a long line so that you can have them compare sizes and shapes of each print ex. Who has the largest print?
- Ask the children to try to pick out their own print
- Make sure you wash all of the children's feet in warm water before putting on their shoes

Evaluation: The children will not want to put their shoes back on. They may need the help of a hand to press firmly enough in the sand to make a deep print. Have the children do this activity with their shoes on as well.

THE GIRL WHO NEEDED GLASSES

Curriculum Area: Language Arts

Objectives: This activity follows the "I'm Special" learning sequence which is intended to make children aware of the differences between them. Some children may have needs that others do not. Language skills will be enhanced through the use of puppets. The children will learn that each of them have different characteristics and sometimes need tools to help them use their sense (vision) to the fullest.

Materials:

- Quiet reading area
- A Hand puppet (girl)
- A pair of glasses

Procedure:

- Have the children sit in front of you in the reading area
- Introduce them to your puppet
- Explain to them that your girl puppet needs to wear glasses so that she can see better
- Show them a pair of glasses and then put them on your puppet's face
- Begin to tell them the story about how the girl needs glasses to see, making up little scenarios to fit the theme. Ex. The girl looks at something but doesn't know what it is. Have a paper bird propped up somewhere in the room where the children can see it clearly
- Have the children tell the puppet what it is that they see
- Put the glasses on the puppet and exclaim "now I can see the bird"
- Use many different approaches, for example, have the puppet ask the children if they would like to try on her glasses
- Allow each child to try them on

Evaluation: The children will enjoy a learning experience through the puppet story. The will participate in trying on the glasses and the older children will be quite receptive to the story. This is a good anti-bias activity. You may want to show the children other styles of glasses such as safety glasses and swimming goggles.

BRUSHING AND GROOMING

Curriculum Area: Music/Social Studies

Objectives: This activity deals with personal hygiene. We will use music as a learning tool. The building of self-esteem will be enhanced through hands on experience and an awareness of one's self.

Materials:

- Hairbrushes, toothbrushes
- Large group area

Procedure:

- Have children sit in a large circle
- Explain that they will be singing a song about brushing their hair and brushing their teeth. Keep the concept of brushing as the focus
- Give each child a hairbrush
- Sing the song melody "this is the way we brush our hair" etc.
- You should be singing and doing the actions at the same time
- When the song is completed and the children have made the gesture to brush their hair you can exchange the hairbrushes for toothbrushes and repeat the song

Evaluation: Most children enjoy using their own brushes to practice good hygiene. They will do a fairly good job of this activity. Continue this exercise at another time using a face cloth for washing hands and face.

FOLLOW THE LEADER

Curriculum Area: Gross Motor/Music Movement

Objectives: This activity will enhance listening and direction taking skills. The children will interact together and depend on one another. We will facilitate learning for spatial and direction concepts. Language will be practiced through the use of words.

Materials:

- Outdoor play area
- Large space for activity

Procedure:

- Take the children outdoors
- Have some of the caregivers follow each other around the yard to demonstrate the activity
- Explain to the children that they are going to play follow the leader
- The caregiver will stand at the front of the line and have the children line up behind her
- Start to walk forward
- Have the children hold on to each other's waists
- Walk around the open play area, sing songs as you weave your path

Evaluation: Toddlers love to play action games. They should be quite receptive to playing this game. Through this activity the children will learn to be aware of others around them. Repeat the same activity holding hands. Show them pictures of animals that follow their leader, ex. Ducks.

FEELINGS

Curriculum Area: Literature

Objectives: There are many aspects to our feelings. We have to teach children at an early age that it is acceptable to express their feelings. Introduce them to many different feelings using the labels given for each expression. They should become aware of their own feeling and learn to recognize the feelings of others.

Materials:

- Quiet reading area
- A book on feelings (if possible or just describe the picture with a quick story)
- Pictures of faces (happy, sad, excited)etc.

Procedure:

- Have the children sit on the floor in the reading area
- Talk in general about feelings
- Show them pictures of happy faces, sad faces etc.
- Read them a story about feelings
- Show each illustration as you read each page

Evaluation: Have the children play out some of the facial expressions for each feeling as you go along. You will have to repeat this exercise many times over the course of your unit in order for the children to fully understand the concept of feelings and be able to recognize them by name. You may want to draw happy faces with the children as another activity.

DRAW A PICTURE OF YOURSELF

Curriculum Area: Language Arts

Objectives: This activity, which continues in the "I'm Special" theme, is designed to encourage children to have a better understanding of self. Encourage activity in this exercise. The children should become familiar with their own individual characteristics. We will encourage curiosity of one's self and develop the concept of symbols.

Materials:

- Paper, crayons
- Art centre
- Small size table and chairs

Procedure:

- Have two to three children at the table at a time
- Have the paper and crayons set out on the table before you begin
- Demonstrate by drawing a picture of yourself while explaining to them what they are going to do
- Ask the children to draw a picture of themselves
- Talk to each child individually about the colour of their hair and eyes as they draw
- When the group has completed the activity hang their pictures on the wall with their names under each one

Evaluation: The concept of this exercise was to have the children focus on "self". You cannot expect a picture of a person at this developmental level. If they are holding a brown crayon to signify brown hair then the activity is a success. They will probably scribble a picture of themselves on the paper. Another activity to encourage becoming self aware would be to draw a picture of a friend.

BEAN BAG GAME

Curriculum Area: Gross Motor

Objectives: This activity is designed to build confidence and self-esteem.   Eye-hand coordination and turn taking will be the focus.

Materials:

- Outdoor play area
- Bean bags and buckets

Procedure:

- Have the children form two lines
- Place a bucket at the front of both lines
- When the children have formed their lines hand the front child the bean bag
- Demonstrate throwing the bean bag into the bucket
- Have each child take a turn and then go to the back of the line
- Continue the activity until each child has had two or three turns
- Encourage and praise each child as they take their turns

Evaluation: This is a good activity for practicing gross motor development. To become competent with throwing skills the children will need a lot of practice. You may want to try this exercise using different throwing techniques (overhand, underhand).

MIRROR REFLECTIONS

Curriculum Area: Language Arts

Objectives: This activity will enhance language development through rhyme. The children will compare likes and differences. The use of song will help development an appreciation for music. Self-confidence will also be a focus for this exercise.

Materials:

- Reading area
- Rhyme song (see procedure)
- Mirror

Procedure:

- Have the children sit on the floor in front of you
- Show them a mirror
- Have them look into the mirror at their reflection one at a time
- Explain to them that you are going to recite a rhyme about yourself
- Hold the mirror in front of each child and sing the rhyme to them
- When you have repeated the rhyme to every child individually, say the rhyme again as a group
- Ask the children some questions, for example, where is your nose?   where are your eyes?
- Rhyme: Look in the mirror

What do you see?
A very nice person
It must be me

Evaluation: Looking in a mirror brings out the curiosity in children. They are quite interested to see themselves in their reflection. You may want to have two of the children look into the mirror together and then ask them questions about their friend's features. This activity will build self-esteem and awareness of one's self.

GROUPING AND SORTING

Curriculum Area: Social Studies

Objectives: This activity will begin to make children aware of the fact that there are many people around them that are from different cultures. They will begin to categorize and group people of their ethnic backgrounds by characteristics. Sorting and matching skills will also be a focus.

Materials:

- Reading area
- Matching sets of pictures of children from other cultures (Asian, African etc.)

Procedure:

- Have the children sit in front of you on the floor in the reading area
- Show them the pictures one at a time
- Lay the pictures on the floor in front of the children
- Ask them one at a time to point at the picture of the child that looks most like them
- After each child has had a turn place all the pictures in front of them again on the floor
- Ask them to match each boy and girl together that look alike
- Continue the game until all of the children have had a turn

Evaluation: Some of the children will need assistance doing the matching activity. This activity is an excellent multicultural learning experience for the children. You may want to add to the activity by taking a picture of a group of people celebrating and have the children try to match the festival with the country and its people. For example, a Greek festival matched with Greece or a group of Spanish dancers with Spain.

WHO IS MISSING GAME

Curriculum Area: Social/Gross Motor

Objectives: This activity emphasizes socialization skills. The children will become aware of the friends around them. They will practice name recognition, association and cognitive thinking skills.

Materials:

- Outdoor play area

Procedure:

- Take the children outside to a large play area
- Explain the rules of the game
- Have the children form a large circle
- Have the children cover their eyes while one of the children is removed from the circle
- When you tell them to open their eyes have them look around the circle for their missing friend
- You will have to help them by naming the missing friend and having them repeat after you
- When they discover who the missing friend is, that child comes back to the circle, they cover their eyes again and another child is removed to hide

Evaluation: The toddler attention span is quite short. They are still at the stage of "I" and "Mine" so it may take some patience to have them realize that there is someone missing. To help with recognition skills play the game with familiar toys.